AMERICAN SLIGO

Adam Rapp

BROADWAY PLAY PUBLISHING INC
New York
www.broadwayplaypublishing.com
info@broadwayplaypublishing.com

AMERICAN SLIGO
© Copyright 2008 by Adam Rapp

Cover photo by Annie Parisse
First printing: December 2008
I S B N: 978-0-88145-390-4

Book design: Marie Donovan
Word processing: Microsoft Word
Typographic controls: Ventura Publisher
Typeface: Palatino
Printed and bound in the U S A

AMERICAN SLIGO was first produced by Rattlestick Playwrights Theater (David van Asselt, Artistic Director; Sandra Coudert, Managing Director; Lou Moreno, Associate Artistic Director), with its first performance on 12 September 2007. The cast and creative contributors were:

ART SLIGO .... Guy Boyd
BOBBY BIBBY .... Matthew Stadelmann
KYLE SLIGO .... Michael Chernus
AUNT BOBBIE .... Marylouise Burke
VICTOR SLIGO .... Paul Sparks
LUCY .... Emily Cass McDonnell
CAMMIE .... Megan Mostyn-Brown

Director ....Adam Rapp
Scenic design .... John McDermott
Costume design .... Daphne Javitch
Lighting design ....Ben Stanton
Sound design .... Eric Shim
Fight choreographer ....Rick Sordelet
Production stage manager ....Jess Johnston
Assistant stage manager .... Zac Chandler
Assistant director .... Dominic DAndrea
Assistant lighting design ....Peter Hoerburger
Press representation .... O & M Co
Production manager .... Kathryn Pierroz

CHARACTERS

ART SLIGO
BOBBY BIBBY
KYLE SLIGO
AUNT BOBBIE
VICTOR SLIGO
LUCY
CAMMIE

a home in suburban Ohio

the present

DEDICATION

Dear Chernus

(The SLIGO'*s)*

(A two-story Midwestern home of moderate furnishings. Things are generally well kept. A dining room with a large dinner table and five chairs, as well as a piano bench with flowers and a votive candle set on it. A china cabinet with old Hummel figurines and a few pieces of decent china. A living room with a sofa, a regular pillow on the sofa with an old white pillow case, a few overstuffed chairs, a La-Z-Boy, a decent-sized T V on a stand, a stereo system with speakers, board games under a coffee table, magazines scattered here and there, a small piano, a large family portrait of a married couple and their two young boys over the piano, a bookcase filled with books. A flight of stairs leading to the upstairs bedrooms. A kitchen, off right. A hallway leading to a back porch. A case of beer in the hallway.)

(Seated at the dining room table are ART SLIGO, *the father, an enormous, vigorous professional wrestler of sixty-three, wearing a fire engine red wrestling singlet, classic black wrestling boots, kneepads, a genuine mullet, and eyes made up like early Ozzie Osborne, and* BOBBY BIBBY, *small, polite, sixteen, their guest, happy as hell to be there. He wears a case around his neck, which contains a digital camera and a white T-shirt that says "I Won the Crazy Train Sweepstakes!" on the front and "The Crazy Train Will Live Forever!" on the back.* KYLE SLIGO, ART'*s youngest son, twenty-six and fully bearded, overweight, discontent but somehow hopeful, is sitting on the sofa in the living room, working on a laptop computer.)*

*(*ART *is staring straight down.* BOBBY BIBBY *is just sitting there, trying to contain his excitement. The piano bench has*

been set opposite ART. *At that place setting is a wine glass with a small votive candle.)*

(AUNT BOBBIE, *early fifties, enters with a big plate of lamb. She works very hard at making others happy but still hasn't yet found her place in the world.)*

(It is late summer, early evening, not too hot.)

AUNT BOBBIE: *(Setting the lamb down)* It's a big night, everyone! A *superbig* night! All the stars are lining up, I can feel it. Kyle, don't pick at the lamb, we haven't said grace yet. *(Exits to the kitchen)* Lisa Del Monte from the March of Dimes Orchid Walk told me that two of the Von Erich brothers are gonna be there. *(Entering with a bowl of corn)* And Governor Mankeiwitz and his adopted Oriental daughter Celia. And a dozen New York City Firemen. *(Exiting to kitchen)* They're comin all the way from the Big Apple and apparently they're gonna be in full firefighting regalia. *(Entering with a bowl of lima beans)* Boots, helmets, the rubber coats. I've even heard that a few of them might be featured on a particular kind of artistic calendar... *(Exiting to kitchen, immediately re-enters with matches)* I always do the lamb medium rare so if anyone wants it more cooked just let me know. There's corn and lima beans, too. Boys?... *(She lights the votive candle)* What are you drinkin Arthur?

ART: Root beer.

AUNT BOBBIE: A & W or Hires?

ART: A & W.

AUNT BOBBIE: Kyle?

KYLE: Water.

AUNT BOBBIE: Brita or Poland Spring? We got both, you know.

KYLE: Water's water.

AUNT BOBBIE: *(To* BOBBY BIBBY*)* Douglas, we got A & W
root beer, Hires root beer, two percent milk, Hi-C
Flashin Fruit Punch, Strawberry Quick, and Mister Pibb.

BOBBY BIBBY: Mister Pibb, please.

AUNT BOBBIE: Tastes like Dr. Pepper but it's not. Don't
let the caramel scent and handsome maroon can fullya.
There's still that little hint of cherry to contend with.

KYLE: His name is Bobby.

AUNT BOBBIE: Oh, what did I call you?

BOBBY BIBBY: Um, Douglas.

AUNT BOBBIE: Geeze, I'm sorry. I'm usually so good
with names. That's why I worked as a hostess at
Al's Steakhouse for so many years—because I knew
everyone who came in through the door, right Arthur?

ART: You were a regular Dinah Shore.

AUNT BOBBIE: Oh, wasn't I, though? Wasn't I just so
exactly that? Good evening, Chester Stanizeuski, your
table for five is just this way. Hi there, Babette Kinsella.
Will you be enjoying the catch of the day? I heard
a rumor that it's red snapper! And Joline Bosano,
doesn't your hair look just stormy! I just love knowing
everyone's name and singing it out to the world.
It's like a little grand song.

KYLE: Did you just use the word grand?

AUNT BOBBIE: I most certainly did, Kyle. Grand
happens to be my word of the day. Yesterday it
was lothario. I'm trying to expand my vocabulary.

KYLE: I didn't hear you use lothario once.

AUNT BOBBIE: I actually used it several times. For
instance, I bandied it about when I spoke to Gib
Tuscadero at the Bakery and again when I deposited
your father's check at the Savings and Loan and I

even found an opportunity to use it on the phone when I was arranging the delivery of the new paneling that's going to freshen up the basement. I said, "Syd Benjamin" —because that's his name, you see—I said, "Syd Benjamin, you handsome-voiced devilfish, thank you for your help, you've been nothing short of a customer service lothario."

KYLE: Do you even know what lothario means?

AUNT BOBBIE: Of course I know what lothario means.

KYLE: What does it mean?

AUNT BOBBIE: A lothario is a showman or a promoter of commercial entertainment ventures. Like your father's business advisor, Johnny Oblongata.

KYLE: That's impresario.

AUNT BOBBIE: Nu-uh.

KYLE: *Yu-huh.* A lothario is a man who attempts to persuade women to enter into sexual affairs with him.

AUNT BOBBIE: Well, you're the one who scored so dang high on those standardized tests they make you take. *(To* BOBBY BIBBY*)* He practically aced the verbal portion and he could've gone to school anywhere in the country. He had scholarship offers galore. In fact one of the schools was in Hawaii where I hear they have wonderful tropical fruit drinks and something called a Polynesian Cheifdom on the Island of Molokai.

ART: I just wanna go on the record as saying that Joline Bosano hung herself with an extension cord back in the Eighties.

AUNT BOBBIE: That's right, she did do that, didn't she? Joline, Joline, Joline Bosano. Poor Joline-where's-the-punchbowl Bosano.

ART: Apparently when they found her she was half purple and there was an army of elephant ants marching out her anus.

KYLE: What's an elephant ant?

ART: I don't know. An ant that looks like an elephant, I guess.

(An awkward pause)

AUNT BOBBIE: You said Mister Pibb, right, Buddy?

KYLE: Bobbie.

AUNT BOBBIE: Oh dear, I did it again.

KYLE: Should we like make him a nametag or something?

AUNT BOBBIE: Well, that's not necessary. *(To* BOBBY BIBBY*)* You said Mister Pibb, right?

BOBBY BIBBY: Yes, please.

AUNT BOBBIE: And you're sure you just want water, Kyle?

*(*KYLE *shoots* AUNT BOBBIE *a look.)*

AUNT BOBBIE: Okay, okay. Gouge my eyes out with your grisly death look why don'tcha? *(She exits to the kitchen.)*

BOBBY BIBBY: Which Von Erich brothers are gonna be there tonight?

ART: Waldo and Lance.

BOBBY BIBBY: Lance Von Erich's gonna be at the Five Flags Civic Center?!

ART: According to the radio spot.

BOBBY BIBBY: That's amazing!

ART: Lance was one of the girliest fighters in North America.

KYLE: Apparently he's not even a real Von Erich.

ART: How do you know?

KYLE: It's on the Internet.

ART: You and that goddamn Internet.

KYLE: What's wrong with the Internet?

ART: I put more faith in frog urine.

AUNT BOBBIE: (*Entering with Mister Pibb, water, root beer*) I've discovered a blistering game of bridge on the Internet. Bridgemaster-dot-com. Take the tour. Baby Blackwood, watch your back good. Gambits galore. Absolutely blistering... Has anyone heard from Victor?

(*No answer*)

AUNT BOBBIE: He said he would be here. I talked to him about it the other day.

(*Still no answer. A buzzer sounds.* AUNT BOBBIE *makes a gesture toward the kitchen, exits.* ART *starts to apply black eye makeup.*)

KYLE: (*To* BOBBY BIBBY) So did they fly you all the way here from Idaho?

BOBBY BIBBY: I took the bus.

KYLE: How long was that?

BOBBY BIBBY: Like two and a half days.

KYLE: That must have been torture.

BOBBY BIBBY: After I got a seat away from the bathroom it wasn't so bad.

KYLE: You win a sweepstakes and they make you take a bus?

BOBBY BIBBY: I didn't mind it so much. It was real scenic.

KYLE: Dad, you should talk to Johnny Oblongata. I mean what kind of *grand prize* is that—making a kid

get on a Greyhound for two and a half days?
Congratulations, come have dinner with Art Crazy
Train Sligo before his historic final match. Hop on a
bus and suffer for sixty hours.

AUNT BOBBIE: *(Popping out from the kitchen)* Grand prize
Kyle. *Grand. (She exits back to the kitchen.)*

KYLE: *(To* BOBBY BIBBY*)* Did you get any sleep?

BOBBY BIBBY: A little. But I've had like five Red Bulls so
I'm cool.

AUNT BOBBIE: *(Entering from the kitchen)* Speaking of
sleeping, I know they're putting you up at the Red Roof
Inn, which is a very respectable establishment with
grand botanical selections in their little lobby area,
but you're more than welcome to stay the night here.
The couch is a paragon of comfort and there's also an
inflatable battering ram.

*(*KYLE *punches himself in the thigh.)*

AUNT BOBBIE: I mean *mattress.*

*(*KYLE *issues a sharp, wordless sound.)*

AUNT BOBBIE: I'll be right back with my homemade
mint sauce. *(She exits to the kitchen.)*

KYLE: Did it cost anything to enter the sweepstakes?

BOBBY BIBBY: Well, the entry form was in Ring Fury
Magazine so you had to buy one of those.

KYLE: How many magazines did you buy?

BOBBY BIBBY: Like four hundred some.

KYLE: And how much is that magazine?

BOBBY BIBBY: I don't know. Maybe like three bucks or
something.

KYLE: *(Punching himself in the thigh)* Dad, he spent
over twelve hundred bucks buying magazines for the

sweepstakes and they put him on a fucking bus! You gotta talk to someone!

ART: I heard ya already! I'll speak to Johnny Oblongata, okay?!

(A strained silence)

BOBBY BIBBY: You totally don't have to. I'm just glad I'm here.

KYLE: Do you have a job?

BOBBY BIBBY: I had one, yeah. I was working concessions at the new multiplex in Cascade. But I had to leave that to come out here.

KYLE: So you quit.

BOBBY BIBBY: Sort of, yeah.

(AUNT BOBBIE enters with mint sauce.)

AUNT BOBBIE: And here we have it, here we do indeed. Aunt Bobbie's homemade mint sauce. Grand, grand, grand. Kyle, have you washed your hands yet? I just put a new thing of anti-bacterial Soft Soap in the upstairs bathroom.

KYLE: I washed my hands, yes.

AUNT BOBBIE: Arthur?

ART: I refuse to wash my hands. In fact I may never wash them again.

BOBBY BIBBY: I washed my hands.

AUNT BOBBIE: Well, I'm just gonna go freshen up and I'll be right back. No smoking at the table now, Kyle. I know how you like to partake of the tobacco vice before you eat. All I ask is that you take it to the porch please.

(AUNT BOBBIE exits. From somewhere in his singlet, ART removes a pack of cigarettes, shows KYLE. KYLE claps twice and the lamp near the sofa goes off. He closes his laptop and

hustles over to the table, takes a cigarette. ART *offers one to* BOBBY BIBBY.)

BOBBY BIBBY: No, thanks.

(ART *produces a lighter, lights his cigarette, tosses the lighter to* KYLE, *who lights his cigarette as well.* KYLE *tosses the lighter back to* ART *and they smoke. After a strained silence:*)

ART: Whaddaya spose a kid like you weighs, anyway?

BOBBY BIBBY: Me?

ART: Yeah, you.

KYLE: *(To* BOBBY BIBBY*)* What do you weigh?

BOBBY BIBBY: Like one-twenty.

ART: Goddamn beetleweight.

BOBBY BIBBY: I actually wrestled one-nineteen on the J V for half the season last year, but I broke my collarbone.

ART: Someone suplexed ya?

BOBBY BIBBY: No. I drove my ten-speed into a plumbing van.

ART: Kyle wrestled for a little while, but he got too fat. Whaddaya weigh now, Kyle?

KYLE: *You're* asking *me* that?

ART: Yeah, whaddaya think you're going for these days, two-thirty, two-forty?

KYLE: I don't know. I don't really think about it.

ART: I would say you might even be pushin two-forty-five.(*To* BOBBY BIBBY)Kyle went to the pro camp for two weeks. Al Snow's operation down in Louisville. Came back with the heebie-jeebies.

KYLE: I didn't come back with the heebie-jeebies, I strained my sacroiliac.

ART: Two hundred forty-five pounds of the heebie-jeebies.

KYLE: Dad!

ART: What? There ain't nothing wrong with it. I'm damn near three-hundred.

KYLE: Yeah, I noticed.

ART: (*To* BOBBY BIBBY) We carry our weight well in this family. (*To* KYLE) Your brother's thin like your mother. He's strong, though. Even with the diabetes he's strong.

KYLE: (*To* BOBBY BIBBY) I strained my sacroiliac, okay?

BOBBY BIBBY: Sure.

(*Awkward pause.* BOBBY BIBBY *removes a digital camera from a case that hangs around his neck.*)

BOBBY BIBBY: Mister Sligo, would you do me the honor?

(ART *cringes, almost retches.*)

KYLE: Um, don't call him Mister.

BOBBY BIBBY: Oh.

KYLE: Or Sir.

ART: I'm not a fuckin choir director.

KYLE: That he is not.

ART: And tell him about Hey, too.

KYLE: Yeah, don't call him Hey, either.

ART: Call me Hey and you might as well call yourself a cab.

KYLE: Call him Crazy Train.

BOBBY BIBBY: Really?

ART: Yeah, call me Crazy Train.

KYLE: He only answers to Dad or Crazy Train.

ART: But I'm not your dad, so don't call me that, either.

BOBBY BIBBY: I totally won't.

KYLE: Your choices are basically Crazy Train or The Great Fuckhead in the Sky.

AUNT BOBBIE: *(Entering, her face made up, carrying a glass of Ocean Spray Light Cran-Raspberry Cocktail)* Watch your language, Kyle.

KYLE: What. It's what they used to call him. Even mom did, didn't she, Dad?

ART: I'd call her Minnetonka Marie cause she was from Minnetonka Minnesota and she'd call me The Great Fuckhead in the Sky. It's what we called each other. She played the piano. She played real well.... She played real well, didn't she Kyle?

KYLE: Yeah, she played real well.

AUNT BOBBIE: By the way, are those cigarettes I see dangling from your lips?

KYLE: Cigarettes? I don't see any cigarettes.

AUNT BOBBIE: Very funny, Kyle. Arthur...

ART: What, it's my house. I'll smoke any damn where I please. And so will my son.

AUNT BOBBIE: Well, at least use an ashtray for heaven's sake.

(AUNT BOBBIE grabs an ashtray from the hood of the piano, sets it on the table. ART puts his cigarette out.)

ART: Kyle...

(KYLE puts his cigarette out, studying AUNT BOBBIE for a moment.)

AUNT BOBBIE: What?

KYLE: Did you just hype up your eyebrows?

AUNT BOBBIE: Did I do *what* to my *who*?

KYLE: Your eyebrows look all hyped up. Did you just put makeup on or something?

AUNT BOBBIE: I freshened up a little, sure. Is it too much?

KYLE: You look like a wench in a Renaissance Fair.

AUNT BOBBIE: I do?

KYLE: Yes. A surly wench with a leg of lamb.

AUNT BOBBIE: Arthur, do I look like a surly wench?

ART: I think you look like Karl Malden in The Streets of San Fernando, but what the hell do I know?

AUNT BOBBIE: *(To* BOBBY BIBBY*)* Do I look like a surly wench?

KYLE: Don't ask him that.

AUNT BOBBIE: *(To everyone)* Should I maybe take some of it off?

(No answer)

AUNT BOBBIE: Arthur?

ART: It's your face.

AUNT BOBBIE: Kyle?

KYLE: Well, you're planning on going out in public later, aren't you?

AUNT BOBBIE: *(To* BOBBY BIBBY*)* If you'll just excuse me for a moment. *(She exits.)*

KYLE: If she starts getting on your nerves just tell her to back off.

ART: Yeah, just tell her to back the fuck off. Say, "Back the fuck off, Aunt Bobbie!"

KYLE: Yeah, just be like, "Back the motherfucking off, Aunt Bobbie!"

ART: "And go get me a beer!"

KYLE: "Yeah, go get me a beer!"

ART: "And a brat!"

KYLE: "A beer and a brat! With sauerkraut!"

ART: "Brats with kraut!" Now that's where the money's at. "Back the motherfucking off!"

KYLE: "Back the motherfucking off."

BOBBY BIBBY: I'll totally do that. I'll totally tell her that! Man! Thanks so much! *(Proffering the digital camera)* Would you do me the honor, Crazy Train?

ART: Sure.

(BOBBY BIBBY rises and crosses to the head of the table, stands next to ART. An awkward moment ensues that has to do with who is going to take the picture.)

ART: Kyle...

(KYLE takes the camera. ART does not stand, remains sitting, a blank expression on his face.)

KYLE: Put your wig on.

(ART does so.)

KYLE: You wanna get one of your belts?

ART: Nah.

KYLE: You should go get one of your belts. It'll look cool.

(ART says nothing.)

KYLE: Make a muscle.

(ART makes a muscle.)

KYLE: *(To BOBBY BIBBY)* You, too.

(BOBBY BIBBY *makes a muscle.*)

KYLE: Smile.

(BOBBY BIBBY *smiles.*)

KYLE: Dad, smile.

ART: I am.

KYLE: No you're not. You look like you're impersonating a national monument.

ART: I am a fuckin national monument!

KYLE: At least show a little teeth.

(ART *shows a little teeth, but doesn't smile. At the last moment,* BOBBY BIBBY *puts his arm around* ART. KYLE *snaps the picture as* AUNT BOBBIE *enters. She is wearing less makeup.* BOBBY BIBBY *and* ART *break from their pose.* KYLE *hands the camera back to* BOBBY BIBBY. AUNT BOBBIE *sits.*)

AUNT BOBBIE: Well, I spose we should say grace. Your brother will get here when he gets here.(*To* BOBBY BIBBY)You're not Jewish, are you? Oh, that probably sounded funny coming out. We got nothin against the Jews as a race. The Jews or the Islamics. I was just wondering if you had special grace needs.

BOBBY BIBBY: I was actually raised Unitarian.

AUNT BOBBIE: Oh, *Unitarian.* What's that?

KYLE: They're sort of like Christians but they don't believe in the Trinity, right?

BOBBY BIBBY: Pretty much.

AUNT BOBBIE: So instead of the father, the son and the holy spirit, what do the Unitarians say?

ART: They say the father, the son, and Captain Guacamole.

AUNT BOBBIE: Oh, they don't either, Arthur.

BOBBY BIBBY: We say a regular grace.

AUNT BOBBIE: *Por ojemplo...*

(Confusion)

AUNT BOBBIE: For example.

BOBBY BIBBY: What, you like want me to say one?

AUNT BOBBIE: Oh, I'd like that very much. The Sligos are a very cultured family, aren't we Arthur?

KYLE: You're not a Sligo.

AUNT BOBBIE: What?

KYLE: You're not a Sligo. You heard me.

AUNT BOBBIE: Well, not technically, but-

KYLE: But nothing. You're not a Sligo. Your last name is Mahoney.

AUNT BOBBIE: But don't you think I'm at least an *honorary* Sligo, bein your mother's sister and all?

KYLE: I don't think so, no.

(An uncomfortable silence)

AUNT BOBBIE: *(To* BOBBY BIBBY*)* You don't have to say grace if you're not comfortable sharing.

BOBBY BIBBY: No I'll totally do it... We should probably hold hands.

(They do so.)

AUNT BOBBIE: Is there an image we should have in our heads? Like a circle of light or a glowing panda bear? I know that some religions use metaphors.

BOBBY BIBBY: Just clear your thoughts.

AUNT BOBBIE: Clear our thoughts. Okay, okay, okay. Arthur, Kyle, clear your thoughts, now... Should we close our eyes, too?

BOBBY BIBBY: Maybe, yeah.

(*Everyone closes their eyes.* BOBBY BIBBY *looks around for a second, does not close his eyes, begins the prayer.*)

BOBBY BIBBY: A circle of friends is a blessed thing; Sweet is the breaking of bread with friends; For the honor of their presence at our board We are deeply grateful... Um, that's it.

(ART *and* KYLE *open their eyes and stop holding hands.* AUNT BOBBIE's *remain closed.*)

BOBBIE BIBBY: You can open your eyes now.

AUNT BOBBIE: Oh, but I don't know if I want to! I'm in such a wonderful place! Look, a mountain goat! And an orchard of blackberries! And there's aurora borealis!

KYLE: Open your eyes, Aunt Bobbie.

(AUNT BOBBIE *does so.* KYLE *stares at her.*)

AUNT BOBBIE: What.

KYLE: I want you to say it.

AUNT BOBBIE: Say what?

KYLE: That you're not a Sligo.

AUNT BOBBIE: Oh, Kyle Christopher, don't be such a kidder.

KYLE: I'm not kidding at all.

AUNT BOBBIE: Arthur...

ART: Come on now, Kyle.

KYLE: Say it!

AUNT BOBBIE: Okay, okay, I'm not a Sligo. Geeze.

KYLE: What are you?

AUNT BOBBIE: What am I? I'm Aunt Bobbie.

KYLE: You're a Mahoney.

AUNT BOBBIE: Well, yeah.

KYLE: Say it.

AUNT BOBBIE: I'm a Mahoney.

KYLE: That's right you're a Mahoney. And don't forget it.

ART: Alright, that's enough, Kyle. Knock it off, now.

KYLE: You knock it off!

(*Awkward pause*)

AUNT BOBBIE: Well, that was just a lovely grace, everyone. Lovely, lovely, lovely. Wasn't it lovely, Arthur? And no Amen or nothin. Pretty risky stuff there...

(ART *and* KYLE *are still tense.* AUNT BOBBIE *starts to serve food and pass bowls.*)

AUNT BOBBIE: So this is exciting! We haven't had a dinner guest in a while! Who was the last dinner guest we had, Arthur?

ART: Bing Crosby.

AUNT BOBBIE: Oh, Bing Crosby—wouldn't that be somethin. That grand smile of his. I just love him in The Road to Hong Kong with Bob Hope and Joan Collins. Nineteen Sixty-two I think it was. Nineteen Sixty-two, the year Marilyn Monroe died. Seriously, though, who was our last dinner guest?

KYLE: It was Mrs Griparis.

AUNT BOBBIE: That's right. Judy Griparis from your mother's book group. She stopped by to drop off Marie's Stephen King novels.

KYLE: Barbara Kingsolver.

AUNT BOBBIE: Who's that?

KYLE: Um, Mom's favorite author. She wrote *The Bean Trees* and *The Poisonwood Bible*. Mom hated Stephen King.

ART: She liked the one where the Plymouth Fury turns into a circus clown with syphilis.

KYLE: Have you been eating paint chips?

ART: ...What's a paint chip?

AUNT BOBBIE: All I know is that Judy Griparis came by to drop off your mother's books and we ate spaghetti and peach cobbler and played Scrabble afterwards and your brother beat everyone by two hundred points.

KYLE: We ate *lasagna* and played *Boggle* and Victor won because he kept cheating but everyone was too drunk on Jack and Cokes to know any different.

AUNT BOBBIE: Kyle, you certainly have an impressive memory. How was Victor cheating?

KYLE: He kept saying that sloog was a word.

AUNT BOBBIE: Well isn't it, though?

KYLE: No.

AUNT BOBBIE: Sure it is. It's a sailing ship, right Arthur? A sloog?

ART: How the hell would I know? Sounds like something that floats in a goddamn toilet tank to me.

AUNT BOBBIE: It's a sailing ship. A sloog of war.

KYLE: That's *sloop*. *Sloop* of war.

AUNT BOBBIE: I might be willing to wager with you on that one, Kyle Christopher.

KYLE: Aunt Bobbie, I guarantee you that a sloop is a sailing ship. In fact, it's a small, armed sailing ship that is larger than a gunboat and carries artillery on only one deck. If there's one thing I know it's vocabulary, you even said it before, right Bobby?

BOBBY BIBBY: Yeah, you said it before.

KYLE: I'm the only one who refuted Victor during that Boggle game but per usual no one paid attention. And at the end of the night he stole thirty bucks out of Mrs Griparis's purse and tried to set her hair on fire.

AUNT BOBBIE: Well, that was an accident.

KYLE: He lit an entire book of matches and held it to the nape of her neck.

ART: Jesus on a fuckin jet ski! Who cares?! For one thing, Judy Griparis smells like men's dirty underthings, and for another she could give two Scandinavian shits about anyone in this house. Someone pass the goddamn lima beans!

(AUNT BOBBIE *passes the lima beans.* ART *turns over the bowl, heaps them all onto his plate, throws the bowl behind him.*)

BOBBY BIBBY: I'll totally play Boggle.

AUNT BOBBIE: (*Moves to pick up the bowl that* ART *threw, takes it into the kitchen, eventually returns*) Well if there's one thing we enjoy here in the Sligo household it's board games. Scrabble. Boggle. Trivial Pursuit. Pictionary. I think my favorite game is Monopoly, the Seventieth Anniversary Edition, of course. I think I've beaten Victor at least twice since we got it. Maybe even three times. And he's so good with that Board

Walk Park Place strategy... Where is that brother of
yours, anyway?

KYLE: He's probably knockin off the Piggly Wiggly
on Pulaski Road again.

AUNT BOBBIE: Kyle...

KYLE: What? He's done it three times since he's been
home. He has a deal with the cashier, kicks her back
twenty percent. I think they're dating.

AUNT BOBBIE: They're dating? Wow. *(To* BOBBY BIBBY*)*
Kyle's older brother was away for a while. He
performed some unsavory acts and wound up in the
penitentiary.

BOBBY BIBBY: What'd he do?

AUNT BOBBIE: Is it okay if I tell him, Arthur?

ART: I don't care.

AUNT BOBBIE: Well, after their darling mother passed,
despite graduating with a degree in economics from the
state university, Victor decided to try and enlist in the
Army because he wanted to go help the boys fight for
freedom and the infusion of democracy in the Middle
East, but the service wouldn't take him because he has
the popular medical condition diabetes, so he got pretty
upset after that.

KYLE: He basically drank a fifth of Wild Turkey and
drove our mom's car through the storefront of the local
Army recruiting office and then proceeded to smear
several pounds of his own feces all over their walls.
He's a real credit to society.

AUNT BOBBIE: Well, he seems to be doing better lately,
don'tcha think, Arthur?

(No answer)

AUNT BOBBIE: I really think he is. He seems so much more, I don't know, I guess *energized* would be the word.

KYLE: That would probably be all the cocaine.

ART: Ken The Grocery Store Kaluka used to do cocaine before his matches. Cocaine and Count Chocula breakfast cereal. Now that guy lives down in Macedonia, Alabama with his invalid mother, the poor sonuvabitch.

AUNT BOBBIE: Well, I don't know nothing about no Count Chocula. I'll tellya, though, I'm certainly glad Victor's found himself a girlfriend. Now both you boys have steadies. Kyle, you got your Cammie with her pretty red hair and moody blue-sky eyes, and now Victor's got the Piggly Wiggly gal. What about you, Nicholas, do you have a little ladyfriend?

BOBBY BIBBY: Bobby.

AUNT BOBBIE: *(As if he'd just called her name)* Yes?

KYLE: He's telling you his name is Bobby. You called him Nicholas.

AUNT BOBBIE: Oh, I must have been thinking of Kermit Johansen's adopted son who does the lawn for us now and then.

KYLE: That's Nigel. And he's black.

AUNT BOBBIE: *(Truly confused)* Nigel...

BOBBY BIBBY: I had a girlfriend but she got lupus and had to move to Alaska.

AUNT BOBBIE: Well, that's too bad. But Alaska, wow. What a wonderful, undiscovered land of brown bears and jousting bull mooses! You must be crushed to have lost your sweetheart to a vast unchartered territory. A girl can do wonders for a boy's outlook, right Arthur?

ART: Roberta, pipe down a little, huh?

AUNT BOBBIE: What?

ART: Just give your pie hole a rest, okay?

AUNT BOBBIE: I don't understand what you're saying,
Arthur. Are you trying to say something?

ART: What I'm saying is that I'd like to eat in silence
for just a minute or two. Even ninety seconds would
be really fucking beneficial at this juncture. Just think
of it as an experiment. Canya do that?

AUNT BOBBIE: Of course. I'm a great fan of these kinds
of experiments with communication. We could maybe
hum, too, if you'd like.

ART: No, no humming, goddammit. Just silence. No
more baloney about brown bears and jousting fucking
bull mooses. In fact, the only person who I'm interested
in hearing speak next is our guest, Bobby. So we'll give
our voices a little break, and then when ninety seconds
or so goes by, the first person to speak is gonna be him,
okay?

AUNT BOBBIE: Shall we perhaps turn the T V on?

ART: No. Nothing gets turned on and nobody talks.
Got it?

(Silence. An unbearable ninety seconds. Eventually AUNT
BOBBIE, who can't stand any longer, starts to urge BOBBY
BIBBY to speak with desperate gesticulations.)

BOBBY BIBBY: Um, I just wanna say that being a
Unitarian isn't weird or anything. It's pretty much the
same as being a Christian except we have barbershop
quartets and fishing trips and sometimes they let you
bring your pets to service.

AUNT BOBBIE: Pets in church?! How wonderful! I mean,
I've always admired the grand collection of farm
creatures arranged in the annual Saint Benedict's

Nativity scenes! The little goats! And the cow with
her hot cocoa eyes! Sometimes there's even a German
school teacher.

(KYLE *punches his leg.*)

AUNT BOBBIE: I mean *Shepherd*!

BOBBY BIBBY: This one guy brought his alpaca once and
it threw up a tennis ball and two dollars in Canadian
coins right on the altar.

AUNT BOBBIE: Oh, well that seems like fun. An alpaca,
huh? It almost sounds Pakistani or somethin. When I
was in high school I knew a boy named Ahmed Hamid
and he was from Islamabad Pakistan and he could
predict changes in the weather because his left
pectoralis muscle would start to flutter. He was a
calculus dynamo and looked just like Omar Sharif
in *Doctor Zhivago*. I danced with him once at the Mill
Valley Midwinter Sock Hop. We slow danced to
Perry Como's *Dream Along With Me. (Singing)*
Dream along with me, I'm on my way to a star
Come along, come along, leave your worries where
   they are...
The Mill valley gals were practically lined up around
the block for him. It was truly a grand night.

(*From offstage we hear:*)

VICTOR: COCKSUCKIN MOTEHRFUCKIN SHIT,
GODDAMNIT!!!

(*Moments later, VICTOR enters. He is shifty-eyed,
early-thirties, trying to hide the fact that he is a bit out
of breath. He also sniffles a lot and thumbs at his nose.
He immediately sits and serves his plate with his hands and
wolfs it down.*)

AUNT BOBBIE: Did you wash your hands, Victor?

VICTOR: I washed them in fly-swarmed bull's blood down at the slaughterhouse. Did you wash yours?

AUNT BOBBIE: Of course I did. I always do.

VICTOR: And did you take your enormous daily cocktail of up-to-the-fucking-minute anti-depressants and assorted caffeinated beverages? No need to answer that. (*To* BOBBY BIBBY) Who are you?

BOBBY BIBBY: Bobby.

VICTOR: Bobby who?

BOBBY BIBBY: Bibby.

VICTOR: Are you from Narnia or something? Is Aslan on his way?

KYLE: He won the sweepstakes.

VICTOR: What sweepstakes?

KYLE: To have dinner with Dad before his final match.

AUNT BOBBIE: They flew him here all the way from Ireland.

BOBBY BIBBY: Idaho, actually. McCall, Idaho.

KYLE: And they didn't fly him. They put him on a Greyhound. Which is basically like being held hostage in South America.

VICTOR: How's your prolific beard doing, Kyle? Does your underage girlfriend enjoy running her delicate little hands through it?

KYLE: She does, yes.

VICTOR: And where might she be this evening? Isn't she planning on attending the electrifying festivities at the Civic Center?

KYLE: No, actually.

VICTOR: Why not? Is the greater state of Ohio monitoring her minor status?

KYLE: She's currently on vacation with her family in Florida.

AUNT BOBBIE: Victor, have you been doing cocaine?

VICTOR: Cocaine? Who told you that?

(No one answers.)

VICTOR: Who fucking said I was doing cocaine?! I wanna know!

(BOBBY BIBBY *flies out of his chair.*)

VICTOR: Jesus Christ you're all useless. Kyle, where's the phone?

KYLE: Am I suddenly the keeper of the phone?

VICTOR: Dad?

ART: How the fuck should I know? Ask your Aunt.

AUNT BOBBIE: I believe it's in the bathroom next to the—

(VICTOR *exits very quickly to the bathroom.*)

AUNT BOBBIE: *(To* BOBBY BIBBY*)* You'll have to excuse Victor. He seems a bit tightly wound right now.

KYLE: Tightly wound? He's totally coked up.

AUNT BOBBIE: You really think so?

KYLE: Oh, come on. Look at how he keeps practically masturbating his nostrils.

AUNT BOBBIE: Art, maybe you should go say somethin?

ART: Like what? Stop bein an asshole? I've tried that one a million times. He is who he is.

AUNT BOBBIE: *(To,* BOBBY BIBBY, *changing the subject)* Do you have a big family back in Nepal-I mean Addis-Ababa-I mean McCall? Any brothers or sisters?

BOBBY BIBBY: It's pretty much just my mom and me.

AUNT BOBBIE: And what does she do?

BOBBY BIBBY: She works at the Lithium springs. Hands out towels and stuff.

KYLE: Your parents divorced?

BOBBY BIBBY: No, my dad died when I was four.

AUNT BOBBIE: Oh, I'm so sorry.

BOBBY BIBBY: No, don't be. He was a dynamiter for a logging company. He broke up a big jam and got trapped underneath. But he saved a pretty big day so he's sort of a local legend. I mean, not a legend like you, Crazy Train, it's nothing like that, but they made T-Shirts and stuff.

KYLE: What was his name?

VICTOR: (From off) Fuck!

BOBBY BIBBY: (Startled) Um, Robert. They called him Rockin Robbie. This is his watch. They found it downriver like a month later.

AUNT BOBBIE: Well, that's practically miraculous! What a wonderful timepiece! And it's still good and reliable, I'll bet. And what about your mother? Did she ever remarry?

BOBBY BIBBY: Nu-uh. She dates this trucker named Kent but he lives with this woman who's in an epic coma and I think it's pretty much a big waste of time.

(VICTOR enters with the cordless phone.)

VICTOR: (Slamming the phone into the cradle) Goddamn cocksuckin battery's dead! Kyle, I need you to give me a ride.

KYLE: No.

VICTOR: C'mon, man. One ride.

KYLE: Where?

VICTOR: Over to Marquardt's house. It'll take you ten minutes.

KYLE: I'm eating.

VICTOR: And you're only getting fatter.

KYLE: Fuck you. I'm not going anywhere right now. It's Dad's big night.

VICTOR: Oh, he doesn't care.

KYLE: Yes he does.

VICTOR: Dad, you could give a rat's ass about all this bullshit, right?

ART: Who said that?

VICTOR: You did. The other day I asked you if you were looking forward to tonight and you said it didn't matter and that you'd rather go to the casino and play Caribbean Stud.

ART: Well, I changed my mind.

VICTOR: What about you, Frodo, can you drive?

KYLE: His name is Bobby.

BOBBY BIBBY: I can drive.

VICTOR: *(To* KYLE*)* Where are the keys?

KYLE: In North America.

VICTOR: *(To* KYLE*)* Give him the keys.

KYLE: No.

VICTOR: Give him the cocksuckinmotherfuckin key's, Kyle!

KYLE: He's Dad's guest! He's not driving you anywhere!

VICTOR: Frodo, come here.

(BOBBY BIBBY *hesitates.*)

VICTOR: Come here, Hobbit!

(BOBBY BIBBY *crosses to* VICTOR.)

VICTOR: Closer.

(BOBBY BIBBY *moves closer.*)

VICTOR: You know, for a little guy, you smell really bad. Did you shit your pants or something?

BOBBY BIBBY: No.

VICTOR: You sure? Maybe you should check. By the way, you got twenty bucks?

BOBBY BIBBY: I only got ten bucks left, but it's for the taxi.

(VICTOR *reaches into* BOBBY BIBBY's *back pocket, produces a Mexican wrestling mask.*)

VICTOR: What's this?

BOBBY BIBBY: My mask.

VICTOR: Put it on.

(BOBBY BIBBY *hesitates.*)

VICTOR: Put it on, Bilbo, or I'm keeping it.

(BOBBY BIBBY *puts the mask on.*)

VICTOR: Who are you supposed to be?

(No answer)

VICTOR: WHO ARE YOU SUPPOSED TO BE?

(*Still no answer.* VICTOR *takes* BOBBY BIBBY's *mask off, hands it to him.*)

VICTOR: Go sit down. (*To* KYLE) Kyle, you got twenty bucks?

KYLE: Not for you.

VICTOR: I so love this family. The Sligo loyalty just oozes out of our pores and soaks directly into the heartland! Such an unmistakable brotherhood!

KYLE: You're the one who got the D U I.

VICTOR: What's that supposed to mean?

KYLE: It means there are consequences. You should've thought about that when you decided to drive Mom's Skylark through the storefront of the Army recruiting office.

VICTOR: Will there be any more life lessons this evening, oh bearded one? If so, I'll go get my spiral notebook! Oh, but wait! I can read about the madness within on your little blog.

KYLE: It's not a blog.

VICTOR: Oh, then I'm mistaken. What is it?

KYLE: It's a serial web posting of a story I'm writing.

VICTOR: It's basically his fucking self-indulgent weekly journal entry.

KYLE: It's serialized fiction, Victor. I'm getting paid three hundred bucks for it.

BOBBY BIBBY: What's it about?

VICTOR: Quote, The Nature of Violence in the Average American Home. Does theatrical violence precipitate actual violence? Or is a bad seed simply a bad seed? unquote. Two brothers: Hector and Louden. Just your average, run-of-the-mill *supersibs*—

KYLE: They're not supersibs, they're just regular brothers. One plays hockey and the other one climbs trees.

VICTOR: Yeah, Louden the gay tree hugger.

KYLE: He's not gay, he has a hot girlfriend!

VICTOR: What the hell kind of name is Louden, anyway?

KYLE: Louden's a name.

VICTOR: Yeah, maybe in some fantasy novel about a professional yodeler.

KYLE: It's a name, Victor! Louden Wainwright, the legendary songwriter!

VICTOR: (Mocking) Oooh, Louden Wainwright, the legendary songwriter! Shall I go douche my legendary vagina?! (To BOBBY BIBBY) Anyway, Louden and Hector—which sounds a lot like Victor by the way—start playing a video game called "The Den" in which you throw your opponent into a hidden booby-trapped lair and deploy a team of wolves, snakes, and lions with the intention of tearing your opponent—in this case—Hector—which-sounds-a-lot-like-Victor—limb from limb. Predictably, the brothers start to get addicted—

KYLE: Predictably?!

VICTOR: PREDICTABLY, KYLE YES! YOU MIGHT WANT TO MAKE USE OF THE LITERARY CONVENTION KNOWN AS SUBTELTY, YOU OBVIOUS MORON! (Back to BOBBY BIBBY) Anyway, Frodo, it's everything in their dreadfully drab mother's power to pull them away from their gaming console. "Boys, dinner's ready!" but they don't come. "Boys, can you help me trolley the recycling to the curb?" But they don't recycle and there will be no trolleying, because they're playing "The Den"! And then in their happy home, supersibs Louden and Hector-which-sounds-a-lot-like-Victor start to enact a *real life* brand of violence on each other. Nothing too crazy yet, though. Mostly just slingshot marbles and the occasional fork in the leg. But be sure to tune in for week three, ladies and gerbilfish, because who knows what on god's greasy earth will happen next? Will Louden the Legend

purchase that crossbow he's been gazing at on the
Internet big gaming site? Will
Hector-which-sounds-a-lot-like-Victor actually drill
those vulcanized razor-sharp steel shark's teeth into the
curved end of his hockey stick? Do tune in, America,
because you won't want to miss it!

(VICTOR *and* KYLE *stare at each other hatefully.*)

BOBBY BIBBY: That sounds really cool, Kyle. Is that on a
website?

VICTOR: www-dot-five-and-a-half-chapters-dot-com.
I think there's a hardcopy somewhere, too, if you'd
prefer to read that.

(*Crazy tension.* VICTOR *lounges on the sofa with a warm
beer that he took from the hallway.*)

AUNT BOBBIE: It's a big night for your father, Victor.
Why don't you come join us?

VICTOR: ...Fine. (*He crosses to the table, sits, starts to tear
into his food.*)

ART: Hey!!!

VICTOR: What?

ART: What the hell do you think you're doin?!

VICTOR: Eating.

ART: Check your fuckin blood sugar.

(VICTOR *stares at* ART *for a second, then goes into a pouch
that he always carries on his person, roots around, removes
medical accoutrement.*)

ART: Whattaya missin?

VICTOR: My glucometer.

ART: Well, where the hell is it?

VICTOR: How the fuck should I know?

ART: Kyle, go get your brother's spare glucometer.

KYLE: Where is it?

ART: In the top drawer of your mother's dresser.

(KYLE *crosses to the living room, grabs his laptop, exits upstairs.* VICTOR *spots the cigarette pack, takes one, lights it, smokes, daring* AUNT BOBBIE *to say something.*)

AUNT BOBBIE: So, Arthur, who are you wrestling tonight, anyway? Who's the unlucky opponent?

BOBBY BIBBY: Kadhim The Syrian Desert Bull. He's fourteen and one, his only loss coming to Ike Candinski The Roman Warlock of Shame. Apparently he can bench press like five hundred and forty pounds.

VICTOR: Sand nigger's prolly hung like a mosquito.

AUNT BOBBIE: Victor—

VICTOR: What! He's a slew-footed, Iraqi sand nigger! Prolly smells like Ayatollah fucking Barbecue.

BOBBY BIBBY: I think he's actually Syrian.

VICTOR: Were you there when he slithered out of his mother?

BOBBY BIBBY: No, I—

VICTOR: I DIDN'T THINK SO!!! But don't worry, Frodo, Crazy Train'll knock the towel off his head and all will be right in America, just like the poster says. Ain't that the skinny, Roberta.

AUNT BOBBIE: Well, gosh, I certainly hope so.

VICTOR: *(Staring at* ART*)* All will certainly be right in America.

(KYLE *returns with the blood sugar monitor, hands it to* VICTOR.*)

KYLE: You're welcome.

(VICTOR *snatches the glucometer, proceeds to check his blood sugar, pricking his finger, smearing blood on a small tab, inserting the tab into the glucometer.* BOBBY BIBBY *watches with keen interest.*)

BOBBY BIBBY: Does that hurt?

VICTOR: Only my soul.

AUNT BOBBIE: *(To* BOBBY BIBBY*)* Victor has to monitor his blood sugar every time he eats. In order for his body to properly process the food he ingests he has to inject the right amount of insulin because his pancreas isn't capable of producing any. See how he's using that device there?

(VICTOR *rolls his eyes, reads the monitor, then uses an insulin pen to stick himself in his side, puts everything back in his medical pouch.*)

AUNT BOBBIE: *(Still to* BOBBY BIBBY*)* The fallacy is that most people think it's about sugar and that the insulin saves you if you have too much cotton candy, or say angel food cake. But, Friend From Afar, the most dangerous thing Victor can do is put *too much* insulin in his body. *Too much* insulin could cause him to go into a coma and possibly suffer worse things such as acute heart failure or even a tragic death conniption.

VICTOR: And then all would *definitely* be right in America.

(VICTOR *starts to eat. Everyone follows suit, eating in silence. After a moment,* AUNT BOBBIE *starts to hum Perry Como, falls quiet.*)

VICTOR: Will someone fucking talk or something?

(Silence)

VICTOR: You got big plans for me? Come on, talk!

AUNT BOBBIE: Well, before you arrived, our guest was telling us how much he loved Alaska—

(VICTOR *quickly pushes away from the table, crosses to the
T V in the living room, turns it on, comes back to the table,
sits, resumes eating.* ART *is clearly perturbed.* AUNT BOBBIE
*rises off her chair, goes into the living room, turns the T V
off.* VICTOR *doesn't respond, continues eating. After* AUNT
BOBBIE *has returned to the table and sat,* VICTOR *rises off his
chair and goes into the living room and turns the T V back
on, crosses back to the table, sits. Silence. Scattered glances.*
BOBBY BIBBY *clears his throat.* AUNT BOBBIE *then rises off
her chair, crosses to the living room, turns the T V off again,
crosses back to the table, sits, sighs as if everything's okay.
No one says anything. Again,* VICTOR *rises off his chair,
crosses to the living room, turns the T V on, crosses back
to the table, sits. Then* ART *stands abruptly, not looking
at* VICTOR, *bounds into the living room, pulls the plug out
of the wall, seizes the T V and exits with it into the garage.
Moments later only the noise of* ART *destroying the T V with
an aluminum baseball bat. Moments later he re-enters with
the bat, drops it on the living room floor.*)

(*Suddenly* BOBBY BIBBY *starts choking. His hands slap the
table, grasp at his throat, slap the table, go back to his throat.
An attempt to communicate the International Choking
signal.*)

AUNT BOBBIE: Oh my God! What? What?!

ART: What the hell's wrong with him?

VICTOR: (*not the least bit fazed*) He's choking.

(BOBBY BIBBY *struggles, hurls himself away from the table,
crashes into things, flings himself into the kitchen, where he
can be heard flailing around.*)

AUNT BOBBIE: He's what?! Oh my god, he's what?!

VICTOR: (*Relaxed*) He's choking, can't you see that?

AUNT BOBBIE: Well, what does that mean?!

VICTOR: IT MEANS HE'S FUCKING CHOKING!!!
JESUS CHRIST!!!

(BOBBY BIBBY *explodes out of the kitchen and into the living
room, holding a dust buster, which is somehow on and
blaring, which he thrusts into his abdomen in an attempt
to dislodge the food trapped in his throat.* AUNT BOBBIE
starts to shriek:

AUNT BOBBIE: HE'S TURNING BLUE! HE'S AS BLUE
AS A BLUEBERRY! HE'S TURNING INTO A
BLUEBERRY!

(VICTOR *pushes away from the table, crosses to* BOBBY
BIBBY, *seizes him, brings him back to the table, and then
executes a very effective Heimlich Maneuver and somehow
steals his watch in the process. A large hunk of lamb flies out
of* BOBBY BIBBY's *mouth, lands dead center in the middle of
the table.* VICTOR *crosses back to his place at the table, sits,
resumes eating as if nothing happened.* AUNT BOBBIE *grabs
the dust buster, turns it off.* BOBBY BIBBY *takes a moment,
stunned, then realizes what just happened and starts to wail.)*

BOBBY BIBBY: I'M ALIVE!!! I'M ALIVE!!! MY BODY...
I'M IN MY BODY...MY TUMMY...AND
MY...EVERYTHING FEELS SO NATURAL...

(BOBBY BIBBY *faints on* ART. KYLE *throws his glass of water
in his face.)*

BOBBY BIBBY: *(Looking around, disoriented)* Where am I?
...Mom? ...Kent? ...Amy?...

AUNT BOBBIE: You're here, Handsome Young Guest.
In the dining room of the Sligo home, right smack dab
in the middle of the United States of America in the
year of our lord two thousand and seven. I'm Aunt
Bobbie and that's Arthur Sligo and this is Kyle Sligo,
and that's Victor Sligo and everything's gonna be okay.
(To VICTOR) You saved his life, Victor. Victor, you
saved his life!!! You're a hero!!!

(The doorbell rings.)

VICTOR: Don't answer it.

AUNT BOBBIE: Oh. Why not?

VICTOR: Just don't.

(The doorbell rings again. No one moves. The doorbell rings again. AUNT BOBBIE *makes a move toward the door.)*

VICTOR: *(To* AUNT BOBBIE*)* Hey! What did I just say?!

AUNT BOBBIE: Well, what if it's someone who needs something?

VICTOR: Not everyone in this miserable fucking world needs something! We're not all desperate and depressed and addicted to revolving, heavily advertised pharmaceuticals.

(The doorbell again.)

*(*KYLE *gets up, goes and answers the door.* AUNT BOBBIE *helps* BOBBY BIBBY *get his bearings, perhaps gives him* KYLE's *glass of water.* KYLE *returns moments later with* LUCY. *She is thirty, sweet, has been crying, makeup smeared.)*

LUCY: Hello everyone. I'm Lucy. Lucy Smith. I work over at the Piggly Wiggly on Pulaski Road. I realize that you're in the middle of a family meal and I'm terribly sorry to interrupt.

AUNT BOBBIE: Well, hello right back at you Lucy Smith. Hello, hello, hello! Here, take a seat, dear.

LUCY: Thank you for the offer, but I was actually hoping I could have a quick word with Victor in a more private setting.

VICTOR: Why are you here? This is my home.

LUCY: I always drop you off here.

VICTOR: You drop me off on the corner.

LUCY: But I watch you walk all the way to your door. Just to make sure you get in okay.

VICTOR: And today you didn't.

LUCY: Yes, that other woman with the 2007 Jeep Grand Cherokee did. I took particular note of its high-performance halogen headlamps and royal blue paintjob. She also had a nice figure and streaks of blue in her hair, which I thought to be unusually stylish considering the color of her Cherokee. Is my car too embarrassing for you or something?

VICTOR: No.

LUCY: Well, I should hope not because I'm actually quite proud of it.

ART: What kinda car is it?

LUCY: A Nineteen Seventy-Seven Chevy Vega Wagon.

ART: Does it have air conditioning?

LUCY: I'm afraid it doesn't. But it's a vintage model and it plays cassette tapes.

ART: If it doesn't have air conditioning I'd have to go with the Cherokee.

AUNT BOBBIE: I read the other day about a Cherokee Chief named Cummacatogue who traveled all the way to London, England in Seventeen Sixty-two to meet King George The Third. Howsabout that, huh?

LUCY: Victor, can I please speak to you in private?

VICTOR: Why did I get born into this miserable world?

KYLE: Go talk to her, Victor. Jesus.

AUNT BOBBIE: I'm quite certain the porch is available.

(VICTOR *pushes away from the table, seizes* LUCY *by the arm.)*

LUCY: Ouch.

(VICTOR *leads* LUCY *off.*)

AUNT BOBBIE: Young love is so romantic.

KYLE: You call that *love*?

AUNT BOBBIE: Oh, they're just quarreling. (*To* BOBBY BIBBY) What about our handsome young guest?

KYLE: You mean *Bobby*?

AUNT BOBBIE: Yes, what about you, were you and your lady friend with the lung cancer very much in love.

BOBBY BIBBY: (*Rubbing his throat*) Um, she has lupus.

AUNT BOBBIE: Oh, lupus. What is that exactly?

ART: Spanish card game.

BOBBY BIBBY: It's an inflammatory condition that affects your joints and organs.

AUNT BOBBIE: Well, that sounds quite horrible and convoluted.

BOBBY BIBBY: Yeah, it sucks pretty bad.

ART: Handsome Tom Johnson died of Dick Cancer.

AUNT BOBBIE: Oh, I'll bet you were very much in love. Very, very much in love with that poor girl with the lupus. What was her name?

BOBBY BIBBY: Amy.

AUNT BOBBIE: Amy. Wow. What a lovely name. I knew a nun named Amy once. Sister Amy of Kansas. She had the brightest smile. Just the brightest, grandest smile. I think names can do that. Affect the way a person looks, ya know? For example, if my name was Celine or Georgette, perhaps I'd have prettier hands. Like the hands of those actresses in the French films of yesteryear. And maybe I'd eat more Mandarin oranges

and play a woodwind instrument. But my name
is Roberta so my hands are more like, well, like
a Roberta's hands and I don't do those things.

(VICTOR *and* LUCY *return. She is calm now, somehow more
at peace.* LUCY *might even be sort of smiling.* VICTOR *kicks*
KYLE's *chair.* BOBBY BIBBY *jumps.)*

VICTOR: Move.

(KYLE *gets up.* LUCY *sits.* KYLE *walks around to the other
side of the table, to the open place setting, starts to sit.)*

ART: You know that's your mother's seat.

(KYLE *crosses to the living room, sits on the sofa.)*

AUNT BOBBIE: Is everything okay, you two?

VICTOR: Everything's perfect.

ART: What was the problem?

LUCY: I'm not sure the dinner table is the proper place.

AUNT BOBBIE: There's no holds barred at this table,
dear. Especially tonight. We've had a wonderful meal.
And a new guest who was on the receiving end of a
valiant, life-saving rescue from Victor. No holds barred,
whatsoever, right, Arthur? So whatever it is, you might
as well let it out.

LUCY: *(To* VICTOR*)* Is it okay?

(VICTOR *nods.)*

LUCY: Well, as you may or may not know, Victor and
I have been seeing quite a lot of each other. We met
while he was waiting in line where I work at the Piggly
Wiggly on Pulaski Road. He was buying Bubble Yum
and Poprocks. We went on a few dates: to the Olive
Garden and to the old Dairy Queen on Caton Farm
Road. Well, things moved a little quicker than I'm used
to. You see I was married in my early twenties and I
have a son who is eight now—his name is Tyler—and

after Tyler's father left, I felt very alone and afraid and
I vowed I would never get involved with a man again.
Tyler is in the third grade now and being raised by a
single parent has been hard on him, but since Victor's
been around he's had a male figure to look up to. They
play catch and paint rocks and make copper etchings
and they've really gotten a lot out of each other and
I think Victor is adjusting quite well and despite his
problems with the law and his diabetes and substance
abuse difficulties as well as the many emotional issues
he's been dealing with perhaps spurred by the death
of his mother, in the few months since his release from
the penitentiary in Marion, we've grown very close.

But this morning my son woke me to tell me that he
had just witnessed Victor leaving our apartment with
his Sony Play Station III console, which was Tyler's
combination Christmas-birthday present. It's an item
that took several paychecks to save up for it and it's
given both Tyler and I hours of fun and mother-son
bonding experiences with games like Dark Cloud and
Grand Theft Auto III.

So I came here not to punish Victor for slipping, as
we all sometimes have to take a step or two back in
order to move forward again, but to let him know that
I support him and that if he returns the PlayStation III,
not only will he be forgiven by Tyler and me, and
welcomed in our home again, but that he'll also grow
from the experience.

And just now while we were discussing this on the
porch he agreed to go find the large African American
man he sold it to on Wexler Boulevard and give him his
money back in exchange for the game. What was his
name again, Victor?

VICTOR: Big Nigga T.

LUCY: Big Nigga T, right. So after dinner, Victor's
agreed to go find Big Nigga T and make things right.

ART: How much did you get for it?

LUCY: A hundred and fifty dollars.

ART: Where's the money?

(No answer)

ART: Did he show you the money, Lucy?

LUCY: Well, no, but he assures me he has it.

ART: Victor show her the money.

VICTOR: Why?

KYLE: Because if she's gonna trust that you're getting her son's PlayStation back for him she should know that you still got the money.

VICTOR: I got it, okay, tubby?!

ART: Where?

KYLE: He probably snorted it up his nose.

VICTOR: Thanks, Kyle. Keep heaping on the brotherly support. And don't stop till I'm buried alive in it.

(ART goes into his bag, removes a money clip with a knot of twenties, counts out ten.)

ART: Lucy.

LUCY: What's this for?

ART: It's two hundred bucks. Take it.

LUCY: But why?

ART: Just take it. Go buy your son another PlayStation thingy cause you ain't never gonna see the other one again.

LUCY: But Victor's going to go get it. He's going to go over to find Big Nigga T on Wexler Boulevard, he promised me.

ART: He's not, though. He's gonna do nothin of the sort. Now take the money and leave please.

LUCY: What did I do? Did I do something wrong?

KYLE: You should just go, you really should.

ART: And if you know what's best for you, you'll stay away from my son. He's no good.

AUNT BOBBIE: Oh, but Arthur—

ART: Something's rotten in him, Roberta, and he'll only make her life miserable.

LUCY: Victor?

(VICTOR *says nothing.*)

LUCY: Will I see you at the Piggly Wiggly?

VICTOR: Do circus ponies poop at the parade?

LUCY: I don't know. Do they?

VICTOR: Sometimes I think they do.

(LUCY *takes the money.*)

LUCY: Okay then. (*She starts to back out of the room*) It was nice meeting you all. (*To* ART) Thank you for the money.(*To* VICTOR) Bye, Victor.

(LUCY *exits.* KYLE *takes his seat at the table.*)

AUNT BOBBIE: Well, she was nice.

(VICTOR *stands and slowly approaches* ART, *puts his hand on* ART's *shoulder.*)

ART: Victor, Victor, Victor...

(VICTOR *makes a strange, beak-like pose with his hand, stares at it for a moment, and then stabs* ART *in the heart with it.*)

ART: What the heck was that?!

KYLE: Dim Mak. Chinese death touch from two hundred B C.

ART: WELL, THAT'S NOT COOL!!!

VICTOR: You're fuckin dead now, fatso.

ART: Where'd he learn that?

KYLE: At Marion.

VICTOR: I picked up stones with the tips of my fingers for four straight months. Thirty-two-thousand stones a day. You know how many stones that is?

ART: No.

VICTOR: WELL, DO THE FUCKIN MATH!!!

(VICTOR *returns to his seat, sits, very grave now. A strained silence.* ART *touches his chest. He might even rub it a little.*)

ART: Dim Mak?

KYLE: Dim Mak, yep. He's done it to me practically every day since he's been home. I must have died like thirty times by now because Victor's practically a Ninja.

ART: *(To* VICTOR*)* You just Dim Makked me!

VICTOR: My guess is you got about three hours left.

(ART *rubs his chest, genuinely scared.* AUNT BOBBIE *changes the mood by clinking on her glass with the end of her spoon.*)

AUNT BOBBIE: So, before we move to the tapioca I was thinkin it might be nice if we shared a reminiscence or two about your father and his wonderful career, how'sabout that? We could do it round-robin style. Pick your all-time favorite reminiscence. Why don't I start us off. *(She takes a moment, turns to* ART. *Clinking her glass)* Arthur, I'll never forget that red satin robe with the golden dragon on the back. You wore it from Nineteen Eighty-Five to Nineteen Ninety-Two, I believe. When you were in the ring and the lights were shining off it, well... well, let's just say that you looked very majestic and handsome. *(Clinking her glass)* Kyle?

KYLE: It's a dead heat for me. (A) —there was that Saturday when you wrestled in the parking lot of the Toys-R-Us in Elderville and you pile-drived Geoffrey the Giraffe into the popcorn machine, and (B) —the Maple Heights Munchkin Massacre when you took on those thirty-seven Hungarian midgets slathered in Crisco.

AUNT BOBBIE: The Hungarian Midgets, yes!

KYLE: *(Flat)* Grand.

AUNT BOBBIE: *(Clinking her glass)* ...Handsome Young Guest?

BOBBY BIBBY: That's easy. It's the Ninth Annual M W W F Red Meat Rumble when you wrestled that Royal Bengal Tiger from Nepal. Everyone thought its muzzle was gonna come off and things got sort of scary but then you tweaked his balls and put him in a Chris Winnebago Sleeper Hold and totally made him pass out...I saw that the night they found my dad. You were in the ring and... Well, the way you handled that Bengal Tiger. That was one of the greatest moments of my life, period.

AUNT BOBBIE: *(Clinking her glass)* Victor?

VICTOR: I have nothing to say about a dead man.

AUNT BOBBIE: *(Clinking her glass)* Arthur?

ART: I don't wanna.

AUNT BOBBIE: Oh come on, be a sport.

ART: No.

AUNT BOBBIE: Well, why not?

ART: Because it's all fake.

BOBBY BIBBY: No it's not, its real. You're just saying it's fake because you're Art Crazy Train Sligo and even though there's seven hundred tons of American

Ethanol hurtling toward the ring at thousands of miles
an hour, when it comes down to it you're humble and
gracious just like the magazines say.

ART: I'm not humble. I'm an asshole.

BOBBY BIBBY: No you're not.

ART: Yes I am. I'm a fuckin asshole. My kids don't even
like me. Victor over there just tried to kill me. You saw
it with your own eyes.

VICTOR: Judging by the way you're turning red, I'd
even say you have about ninety minutes.

BOBBY BIBBY: Kyle, isn't your dad humble and gracious?

KYLE: Um, he's sort of an asshole.

BOBBY BIBBY: It's red-white-and-blue blood thunder and
thousands of pounds of flesh-torn nightmares! You say
it yourself every Saturday morning!

ART: That's a used car commercial! Some idiot wrote
that on a piece of poster board!

AUNT BOBBIE: I like that commercial. You look so
vigorous, Arthur. So vigorous and...well, vigorous.

ART: We're quarter-ton clowns with an appreciation
for stunt work. We're told what's gonna happen by the
promoter when we're in the locker room, if there even
is a locker room. I'll say it once and I'll say it right here
and now: Pro Wrestling's been the biggest pain in the
ass of my life. I shoulda stayed a shoe salesman.

BOBBY BIBBY: But what about all those great moves?
Like the Hurtgen Forest Ax Handle and the Mongolian
Stew Warrior Chop. Or the Flying Clothesline of Doom,
what about the Flying Clothesline of Doom?! Or your
signature El Kabong, man? You have the best El
Kabong in the M W W F!

ART: Those are just moves, Bobby! Things a body does.
The Shining Wizard and the Mongolian Stew Warrior
Chop and the Flying Clothesline of Doom and the
Colorado Stinkface—it's choreography! We might
as well be ballerinas in tutus! And all those goddamn
phony holds, no real resistance comin back at you.
The Sunset Flip and the Oklahoma Sausage Roll. Phony
baloney! The Rana and the La Casita. Pure bullshit on
toast! Sure, I could run into you in a *parking lot* and put
you in a halfway decent Colombian Crucifix. I could
see you at the friggin *fairgrounds* and throw a Pensacola
Chickenwing on you. Or a Fujiwara Armbar for that
matter. I'm damn near sixty-three years old and I got a
better Tongan Death Grip than guys half my age. I have
a top-of-the-line Canadian Backbreaker and I'm not
even Canadian! You want an Octavian Octopus Hold,
I'll show you one right there in the living room! I'll
throw the goddamn sofa through the wall and ruin
your life with the Tony Hiawatha Tree of Woe! But
it would be fake, *(Removing his wig)* don't you get it?

KYLE: Dad.

ART: What, Kyle? This is the sum of my life. I got a pile
of medical bills, arthritis in my hips, a car with a broken
down transmission, and a knucklehead ex-con son.

VICTOR: And don't forget about your dead wife.

(ART glares at VICTOR a moment.)

ART: *(Putting his wig back on)* If you'll excuse me,
I'm walkin to the Civic Center. And don't nobody
follow me, I wanna be alone! *(He rises, struggles for
a moment, has to push off the table to keep his balance.)*

AUNT BOBBIE: You okay, Arthur?

(ART struggles.)

KYLE: Dad, you okay?

ART: My chest feels funny.

KYLE: Well, sit back down.

ART: No. Just gimme a minute.

AUNT BOBBIE: Need a glass of water or somethin, Arthur?

ART: Leave me alone.

KYLE: Dad, really.

ART: I'm walkin to the goddamn Civic Center! And like I said, don't follow me!

(ART *rights himself, slowly gets his balance, pushes away from the table, exits.* VICTOR *sings Taps.* ART *stops, looks back at* VICTOR, *then completes his exit.* AUNT BOBBIE *follows him down, stops, watches him exit across the porch, turns crosses back to the dining room.*)

AUNT BOBBIE: What I think Arthur was trying to say, Benny, is that it's really just a lot of fun.

KYLE: Jesus Christ, it's BOBBY! Fucking BOBBY, okay?! What if I called you Shirley. Or Bula?

VICTOR: Or Kenneth.

BOBBY BIBBY: *(To* AUNT BOBBIE*)* You can call me whatever you want, really.

KYLE: No she can't, bro! Because your fucking name is Bobby and that's what she's gonna call you! Half the time she calls me Kevin. Or *Kelvin.* And it's Kyle.

AUNT BOBBIE: Well, you do have a cousin named Kevin.

KYLE: Yeah, but *Kelvin*? Where does *that* come from?

VICTOR: Too much daytime television interspersed with commodified pharmaceuticals. What's the new one you've been takin—Gibraltar?

AUNT BOBBIE: Cymbalta. And it's been helping quite
a lot so if you're trying to embarrass me in front of our
guest, it's not going to work.

VICTOR: Cymbalta, right. It's probably why you sweat
so goddamn much. Not to mention the constipation.
You should hear her on the toilet, Bobby, it's like
listening to a polar bear giving birth. All she does
is watch The fucking *Medium* and hide in the garage
and cry and sit on the fucking toilet all day. Oh, John
Edward, channel the spirit of my dead sister in your
slightly effeminate, ghost-tracking tenor. Give me a
false sense of hope where there is none. Hypnotize
me with those dazzling blue eyes of yours.

AUNT BOBBIE: It's called *Crossing Over With John
Edward*, not *The Medium*, and his eyes aren't blue, they
happen to be hazel! And I think it's a very important
show! And for you to sit there and poke fun at my
spiritual relationship with your mother it's, well, let's
just say it's quite small of you, Victor William Sligo!

VICTOR: You know what, Aunt Bobbie? In the end
you're just like the rest of us really. Dad, Kyle, Elijah
fucking Wood over there. And me too.

AUNT BOBBIE: And what's that, Victor?

VICTOR: You're just a sad, pathetic sack of shit.

(AUNT BOBBIE *almost throws a glass at* VICTOR, *but can't,
splashes water on herself. He laughs. She cries.*)

AUNT BOBBIE: How could you have turned out to be
such a cruel person?! Your mother would be horrified
by the things you say!

VICTOR: (*Standing, fast and furious, in her face*) Oh, go
sit on a fucking pencil, you desperate bag of bones!
Or better yet, go take some more Hoodia, the new
breakthrough in weight management! The African
plant that helps fight fat! Better scurry off to your little

laptop! Check the email. You never know what you could be missing, Roberta532@hotmail.com! Oh, that's right, but you've maxed out your Capitol One card buying all your bullshit off the Internet!

AUNT BOBBIE: *(Not backing down)* I made apple pie with Splenda, especially for you, Victor! Apple pie with *Splenda*!

VICTOR: Why don't you go sit on it! It might do you some good down low!

AUNT BOBBIE: *(Still toe-to-toe)* Well, maybe I will go sit on it, Victor, you cruel, cruel, mean-spirited person. Maybe I'll sit right down on it and make a big fat number two in honor of your bitterness. But before I do, I just have one more thing to say and it's this: I am *honored* to be a member of this family. Yes, *honored*. Despite your hatred for me. Despite the embarrassment you no doubt suffer. Despite all the names you call me and the little sideways jokes. I am truly honored! *(She exits to the kitchen, returns moments later with the pie she'd made for VICTOR, sets it on the table and then exits upstairs.)*

(A silence)

BOBBY BIBBY: Your father's a great man, Victor.

VICTOR: Is he?

BOBBY BIBBY: Crazy Train's done so much for so many people.

VICTOR: Has he?

BOBBY BIBBY: Yeah, he's a hero. He gives us hope. What can you do?

VICTOR: I can make you a sandwich. Would you like a sandwich because I'd be happy to make one especially for you, Frodo.

BOBBY BIBBY: No, thanks.

VICTOR: You just let me know... Kyle, I'm gonna kill you later.

KYLE: Great.

VICTOR: You know how I'm gonna do it?

KYLE: No, but why don't you tell me.

VICTOR: Well, first I'm gonna cut you with Dad's straight razor. A short, surgically controlled laceration along the carotid artery. Just long enough to almost be serious. I'll put a compress on it now and then so the arterial pressure won't get too out of control. But I'll be sure to let you lose enough blood so you get really weak and dry in the mouth; so that that strange taste of iron and cotton starts to make you hallucinate about things that live and don't live in trees. And then I'll take a few days and nurse you back to health. Comfort. D V Ds and easy-listening rock. A meal here and there. Coconut water to re-hydrate your fat body. And you'll be thankful. And then I'll take a picture and you'll smile because of the gratitude. And I'll leave the beard alone. I might even brush it a little so it gets soft and fleece-like. Then I'll send the picture to your little girlfriend. But I'll cut the head off and send that portion independent of the body. It'll be like a puzzle for idiots. And then I'll be friendly and let you like me again. We'll play Scrabble and I'll let you have all the triple word squares. I'll even slide my X over to you when you aren't looking. Maybe even a J. And then I'll confiscate your cell phone and as soon as I see Cammie's number come up I'll cut your throat with that same straight razor, but much sharper now, and I'll answer the phone and hold it under your nose so Cammie can hear the almost screams gurgling from your blood-flooded throat; the *not-quite* Help me's drowning in your lungs. And then as soon as you've been totally bled dry I'll probably soak you in kerosene and set you on fire in the old canoe that's hanging in the garage.

KYLE: Thanks, Victor. I love you, too. (*To* BOBBY BIBBY) You ready to go?

(KYLE *and* BOBBY BIBBY *rise and start to exit.* BOBBY BIBBY *now has his backpack.*)

KYLE: (*yelling up the stairs*) Aunt Bobbie, we're leaving, so if you want a ride come now... Aunt Bobbie!

(AUNT BOBBIE *appears at the foot of the stairs. She's wearing pajamas.*)

AUNT BOBBIE: I'm just gonna stay here. Go to bed early. You boys go. I'm suddenly so tired.

KYLE: Suit yourself.

BOBBY BIBBY: Can I have my watch back, Victor?

VICTOR: No.

(KYLE *crosses to* VICTOR, *seizes his arm, removes* BOBBY BIBBY'S *watch, hands it to* BOBBY BIBBY, *stands over* VICTOR.)

KYLE: (*To* VICTOR) At least turn on the radio and listen to the match. Mom would want that.

(KYLE *and* BOBBY BIBBY *exit.* AUNT BOBBIE *eases into the kitchen.*)

AUNT BOBBIE: Victor?

VICTOR: Go to bed.

AUNT BOBBIE: Can I just say one thing?

VICTOR: What.

AUNT BOBBIE: I'm sure you don't remember this, but when you were a little boy, maybe four or five years old, I used to take you to Gladiola Park and put you on the swing. And I'd swing you and swing you and you'd smile and hold on for dear life. Just you and me at the park. Your mom was back here taking care of Kyle because he'd had a scare with the chicken pox. You had such a wonderful smile, Victor. So grand and wonderful. And sometimes you would kiss my cheek and tell me you loved me. And I used to wish that you were my boy. I really did. You would just swing and swing and swing. Those were some of the happiest moments of my life, Victor. Truly some of the happiest moments.

(VICTOR *says nothing.*)

AUNT BOBBIE: Well, good-night then.

(AUNT BOBBIE *crosses to the coffee table, sets the pie down, then turns, exits to her room.* VICTOR *sits there for a moment and then seizes the phone, dials a number, waits.*)

VICTOR: *(Into phone)* Hey, Lucy? It's me, Victor. Hey. Whattaya doin?... Will you come get me... I know, but—... *(He starts to cry.)* Please? ...Oh, come on, Lucy, I don't know what I'm gonna do... Yes! ...Please come and get me... Well, fuck you!!! Fuck you, you fucking dumbass checkout girl cunt!!! Go fuck your cash register!!! And tell your idiot son I hate him, too!!! *(He slams the phone down, cries for a moment. He then pinches the meat between his eyes and then quickly crosses to the sofa, pulls the pillowcase off the pillow, crosses to the china cabinet, starts to fill the pillowcase with the few pieces of valuable china.)*

(VICTOR *then goes into the kitchen, re-enters a moment later with a small, portable T V, puts it in the pillowcase. He then takes the cigarettes off the table, puts them in the pillow case. He then takes a crystal dish filled with candy from the top of the piano, puts it in the pillowcase. He then tilts the family photo on the wall, then pulls the dining room curtains down, then steals some Hummel figurines off the bookcase, then an old trophy football, puts all of it in the pillowcase, then*

*crosses to the living room, turns the stereo receiver on, tunes
in to the wrestling match. The announcer goes on and on
about the career of Art Crazy Train Sligo and what he's
meant to the M W W F, which is punctuated by "And here
he is now!" Just as the crowd starts to roar, he turns it off,
unplugs the receiver, pulls it out of the rack, stuffs the
receiver into the pillowcase, sets the pillow case on the floor
and then quietly ascends the stairs, disappears upstairs.)*

*(The sound of the screen door opening and closing on the
front porch. From the hallway we see* CAMMIE CRESTWOOD,
KYLE's *girlfriend. She is seventeen, redheaded, blue-eyed,
carrying a small duffle bag, a little scared. She wears a
white tank top with Mickey Mouse on the front, blue jeans,
running shoes.)*

CAMMIE: Kyle? ...Kyle?

(Just as CAMMIE *crosses the threshold of the dining room,*
VICTOR *appears at the head of the stairs holding two gold
championship wrestling belts. He descends the stairs quickly,
with light feet. Just as he reaches the foot of the stairs he and*
CAMMIE *see each other, stop. No one moves.)*

CAMMIE: Victor.

VICTOR: Hey, Cammie. What are you doing here?
I thought you were on vacation.

CAMMIE: I am. I mean I was. Is Kyle around?

VICTOR: He's at the Civic Center.

CAMMIE: Oh, right. Your dad's big night.

VICTOR: Dad's big night, yep.

CAMMIE: Why aren't you there?

VICTOR: Kyle will be back in a little while. You can
hang out here. With me.

CAMMIE: What are you doing with those belts?

VICTOR: I was gonna put em on. Wanna put one on with me? Crazy Train lets us wear em. It's real fun. Here.

(VICTOR *proffers one of the belts, takes* CAMMIE's *book bag off for her, sets it down, hands her the belt.*)

CAMMIE: Heavy.

(VICTOR *puts one of the belts on as well.*)

VICTOR: It goes good with your shirt. Mickey.

CAMMIE: That's where we were. Disney World.

VICTOR: The Magic Kingdom.

CAMMIE: Yeah, it's wack, I know.

(*An awkward pause*)

VICTOR: Here. Let's sit on the sofa, why don't we?

(VICTOR *smiles, gestures toward the sofa. They start to cross toward it when a cell phone starts to go off.* CAMMIE *quickly crosses to her bag, removes a cell phone.*)

CAMMIE: Shit!

VICTOR: Who is it?

CAMMIE: My mom. (*She turns the phone off.*)

VICTOR: Are you on the lam, Cammie?

CAMMIE: Sort of, yeah.

VICTOR: The Cammie lam... Come back.

CAMMIE: (*Referring to the championship belt*) Can I take this thing off? It's really heavy.

VICTOR: Keep it on. We're like king and queen. Sit, my little clack dish.

CAMMIE: What's a clack dish?

VICTOR: It's Shakespearean for noblewoman.

(CAMMIE *hesitates, crosses to the sofa sits.* VICTOR *claps twice, turning the lamp near the sofa on. Startling her as well. He crosses to* AUNT BOBBIE's *chair at the dining room table, turns it toward her, sits. The sound of a police siren going by, fading in the distance.*)

VICTOR: So you didn't enjoy Disney World?

CAMMIE: No it was pretty cool actually.

VICTOR: What was your favorite part?

CAMMIE: I'd have to say Peter Pan's Flight.

VICTOR: Ooh, peter Pan's Flight. Tell me about it.

CAMMIE: Well, you sort of like fake sail in this pirate ship to Nevernever Land. It starts in Wendy's bedroom and then you set off and you go over Big Ben and London Bridge and it ends with Captain Hook battling a crocodile. It sounds totally gay but it's actually pretty bad-ass if you're on shrooms.

VICTOR: Were you on shrooms?

CAMMIE: Yeah, I met this guy by Cinderella's Golden Carousal and he hooked me up with a few stems.

VICTOR: What was his name?

CAMMIE: He said his name was Mustafa but I didn't believe him cause he was this total suburban metrosexual white guy in an Abercrombie and Fitch college Tee.

VICTOR: Did you ride Space Mountain?

CAMMIE: I really wanted to but I couldn't.

VICTOR: Why not?

CAMMIE: Well, that's sort of why I'm here and I'm not trying to be a bitch but it's classified information.... Why are you looking at me like that?

VICTOR: How am I looking at you?

CAMMIE: Like you know something?

VICTOR: Do you think I know something?

CAMMIE: I don't know, do you?

VICTOR: You tell me.

CAMMIE: Well, what could you possibly know?

VICTOR: I don't know. What could I possibly know? Are you...smuggling diamonds?

CAMMIE: No.

VICTOR: Emeralds?

CAMMIE: No.

VICTOR: In the process of delivering the new Al Qaeda training manual?

CAMMIE: God no. That's gross.

(VICTOR *produces a handkerchief, blows his nose, shows her. It's all bloody.*)

VICTOR: No, that's gross. (*He starts to cough convulsively, almost falls out of his chair, regains his composure.*)

CAMMIE: Are you okay?

VICTOR: I'm fine. Why?

CAMMIE: Well, Kyle said you were—

VICTOR: Kyle said what.

CAMMIE: No, nothing. He just said you had a lot of issues.

VICTOR: What kind of issues?

CAMMIE: Like health-related things. And how it makes you different. And he told me how you were in jail for a while. But don't get me wrong, Kyle totally loves you. He like worships you.

VICTOR: Does he?

CAMMIE: Yes. You're like his hero.

VICTOR: Am I?

CAMMIE: Yeah. He goes on and on about how smart you are and how you went to school on a full-ride and almost quit because you were like too smart for your professors and how you were this kickass football player in high school and you had scholarship offers but you couldn't take them because you got diagnosed with diabetes and how you read all these complicated novels and how great you are at the *New York Times* crossword puzzle and how you can like finish the Saturday and Sunday ones in under an hour and how you were the one who really stood by your mom when she was sick, how you helped her through the chemo and read to her after she went blind and how everyone else was afraid of her because of how the tumors made her face all distorted but you were the only one who didn't freak out...I mean, I was at her memorial service and you read that poem about her hands and it made everyone cry. I could go on. He really does worship you.

VICTOR: Do you worship Kyle?

CAMMIE: Me? No. I mean I love him, but I don't *worship* him. I don't worship anyone. Not even my parents.

VICTOR: I could have played football in college. I could've done whatever I wanted. I could be the next president of the United States... *(Crossing to her on the sofa)* Hey, you don't have a car do you?

CAMMIE: My parents' Thunderbird's at home but I don't have the keys.

VICTOR: Is there a spare set?

CAMMIE: Yeah, but it's in the house and I can't break in cause the alarm will go off.

VICTOR: Would you like to do some cocaine with me? I only have a little left but I'd be happy to share it with you.

CAMMIE: Um, I've never done cocaine.

VICTOR: It's really great. It's like jumping off the high dive and then getting on a motor cycle.

CAMMIE: I don't like motorcycles. My uncle got killed on one.

VICTOR: What if it was a motorcycle made of Nerf?

CAMMIE: I better not.

VICTOR: Would you mind if I did a little by myself?

CAMMIE: You're not gonna freak out or anything are you?

VICTOR: Only in the best possible way. (*He removes a small plastic packet of coke, taps the corner, digs his fingernail into the bag, snorts it, does it again, rips the bag open, rubs the dust on his gums, makes a face, flings the bag away.*)

CAMMIE: I heard it burns. Does it burn?

VICTOR: Only my soul.... Hey, let's play a game. Let's play The Put Your Hand On My Head Game. It's real easy. You put your hand on my head. And then I put my hand on your head. It's actually one of my favorites. You might like it, too. Come on, you go first.

CAMMIE: I don't know.

VICTOR: Cammie, don't be a little girl now. Come on.

CAMMIE: Okay, but if it gets weird I'm stopping.

VICTOR: Totally your call... So let's stand.

(*They stand.*)

VICTOR: And face each other.

(They face each other. VICTOR *adjusts* CAMMIE's *shoulders so they're squared to his. He then extends his arm to measure her.)*

VICTOR: All children must be forty-four inches to enjoy this ride. *(Placing his arm down)* Now reach your hand out and place it on the top of my head.

CAMMIE: My right hand or left hand?

VICTOR: Doesn't matter. Whatever you're more comfortable with.

*(*CAMMIE *hesitates with her left, then uses her right, places it on* VICTOR's *head.)*

VICTOR: How's that feel?

CAMMIE: Okay.

VICTOR: Do you like my hair? I conditioned it today. I use Prell.

CAMMIE: It feels soft.

VICTOR: Now I'm gonna put my hand on your head. Ready?

CAMMIE: Uh-huh.

VICTOR: Here we go. *(He places his hand on her head.)* Cool, right?

CAMMIE: Uh-huh.

VICTOR: It's like we're blessing each other.

CAMMIE: It is, sort of.

VICTOR: Now the big move, Cammie Cameroon. Let's make The Circle of Life.

(They start turning a circle.)

VICTOR: Can you feel the love tonight?

CAMMIE: Sure.

VICTOR: Hi.

CAMMIE: Hi.

VICTOR: Hello.

CAMMIE: Hello.

VICTOR: Welcome to Space Mountain. Yay!!! (*Singing*) It's a small world after all, it's a small world after all... Don't take your eyes off me now.

CAMMIE: I'm not.

VICTOR: Do you love my little brother?

CAMMIE: I think so.

VICTOR: With all your heart?

CAMMIE: Sure.

VICTOR: If he asked you to marry him, would you do it? Would you cook and clean for him and spread your white hairless legs in the middle of the night?

CAMMIE: I'm getting dizzy.

VICTOR: Answer the question. If Kyle asked you to marry him, would you do it?

CAMMIE: I think I'm gonna be sick.

(CAMMIE *drops to her knees, grabs the pillowcase, vomits.* VICTOR *removes his wrestling belt, drops it on the floor.*)

CAMMIE: Sorry.

VICTOR: It's okay, Cammie. You can get sick all you want.

(CAMMIE *vomits again.* VICTOR *exits to the kitchen, steals her cell phone out of her back pack on the way, leaves her retching on the floor. Moments later he returns with a glass of water, sets it on the dinner table. She looks back, sees the water, rises off the floor, crosses to the table, sits. She takes a drink of water.*)

(VICTOR *places a vial of insulin and a hypodermic needle in front of her at the table. Then, in one swift move, he removes his shirt and jacket, so he is naked from the waist up, save for his silver medical diabetes chain. He then sits and starts eating the pie.*)

CAMMIE: What are you doing?

VICTOR: Eating pie.

CAMMIE: Isn't that bad for you?

VICTOR: It depends on my blood sugar.

CAMMIE: Don't you have to check it first?

VICTOR: Yeah, but I'm not going to this time.

CAMMIE: Why not?

VICTOR: Because I'm trying to kill myself.

CAMMIE: You are?

VICTOR: Affirmative.

CAMMIE: Well, don't.

VICTOR: Too late. I'm already starting to die.

CAMMIE: That's crazy, Victor! You're fucking out of your mind!

VICTOR: In about three minutes my blood sugar is going to spike so high that I could have a heart attack, unless I put some of that insulin in my body.

CAMMIE: So put some in your body.

VICTOR: Nope.

CAMMIE: Why not?

VICTOR: Because I'm trying to kill myself.

CAMMIE: Why?

VICTOR: Because you puked in my pillowcase, Cammie, and I no longer have a reason to live. You see, I was going to sell all the items in the pillowcase so I could buy some more cocaine from Big Nigga T on Wexler Boulevard. But Now I can't because they're covered in your grossness!

CAMMIE: Then I'll clean the stuff off.

VICTOR: Too late.

CAMMIE: Victor, stop fucking around. You're scaring me.

VICTOR: Watching someone kill themselves with pie is scary. Welcome to America, Cammie. Enjoy the ride.

CAMMIE: Put some insulin in you!

VICTOR: *I'm* not gonna do it.

CAMMIE: Then I'll do it. Tell me what to do.

VICTOR: See that little vial of clear liquid?

CAMMIE: Uh-huh.

VICTOR: And see that little hypo?

CAMMIE: Uh-huh.

VICTOR: Take the hypo and suck all the clear liquid out of the vial and then stick it in my side.

CAMMIE: Okay.

VICTOR: But you're gonna have to do it at least a coupla times cause of all this pie I'm eating.

CAMMIE: Well stop eating it!

(CAMMIE *tries to snatch the pie but* VICTOR *is too quick.*)

VICTOR: You're losing time, Cammie Crestwood With The Nice Red Hair. You got about another minute before I start foaming at the mouth.

(CAMMIE *takes the hypo, punctures the top of the vial, draws the insulin.*)

CAMMIE: Like this?

VICTOR: Yep. Just like that. *(He stands very close to her)* Now stick it in my side and push on the plunger. You can go right through the skin.

(CAMMIE injects VICTOR. He jerks to scare her and she screams.)

CAMMIE: Did that hurt?

VICTOR: Only my soul. Now you're gonna have to do it at least three more times.

CAMMIE: I don't know if I can.

VICTOR: Then things are gonna get real interesting in about forty-five seconds.

CAMMIE: Fuck! Okay, again then.

(CAMMIE does it again, repeating the same process as before, drawing the insulin into the syringe and injecting VICTOR in his side.)

VICTOR: At least two more times, Cammie. Maybe even three.

CAMMIE: Stop eating, then!

(VICTOR throws the pie. The insulin is starting to disorient him. CAMMIE fills another hypo full of insulin and sticks him again. And then goes to work on yet another hypo, fills it with insulin, sticks him again. He jerks oddly. She screams.)

VICTOR: Enough. *(He sits, holding her arm. He picks up the vial of insulin, holds it up to the light.)*

VICTOR: Wow. Nice work. *(Sets the vial down)* Can you play the piano?

CAMMIE: Not really.

VICTOR: Come on, everyone can play a song or two. Please? Just one little song? ...Play!

CAMMIE: Okay. *(She crosses to the piano, starts to play something like* Heart and Soul. *She messes up, starts over. She messes up again, stops.)*

VICTOR: Keep going.

(CAMMIE starts again. VICTOR crosses to the piano, muttering strangely, the insulin needle hanging out of his left side. He does not sit, but kneels down beside her, begins playing, but discordantly. She stops.)

VICTOR: No stop.

(CAMMIE starts again. VICTOR bangs on the keys. She stops. He can't seem to focus. She gets up very quickly, to the door, but he cuts her off. She goes into the living room. He approaches her, very disoriented now.)

VICTOR: Call it.

CAMMIE: Call what?

VICTOR: You have to call it.

CAMMIE: Call what?! Victor!!

VICTOR: B-thirty-two. Call it.

(VICTOR is on his knees, pawing CAMMIE oddly.)

CAMMIE: Victor, call who?! Call Kyle?! Call the hospital?! Should I call the hospital?!

VICTOR: Tell me you love me.

CAMMIE: I love you Victor.

VICTOR: Please marry my brother. Please, please, please...

CAMMIE: Okay, okay, I'll marry Kyle.

VICTOR: *(Standing now, totally disoriented)* I gotta go pee... Math circle...bullfinch...cookie truck...

(VICTOR starts to take his pants down. He falls backwards onto the sofa, so that it looks like he is sitting oddly,

muttering unintelligibly. CAMMIE *moves to the kitchen table, seizes the hypo, starts to draw more insulin.)*

(The sound of the porch screen door opening and closing. KYLE *rushes into the room. He is hyperventilating, trying to stay cool.* BOBBY BIBBY *eases into the room behind him.* CAMMIE *is hysterical.)*

KYLE: Cammie.

CAMMIE: Hey, Kyle.

KYLE: What are you doing here? I thought you were in Orlando... Why are you wearing my dad's championship belt?!

CAMMIE: I love your beard, Kyle. I really do love your beard.

KYLE: My beard? What?! What the fuck is going on?!

CAMMIE: I came all the way from Orlando. I took a bus. What's wrong with you? Why are you crying?

KYLE: My dad had a stroke. He's in the hospital. Victor, Dad had a stroke! We gotta go to the hospital! What's wrong with him? Why are you holding that needle?

CAMMIE: He kept telling me he needed insulin.

KYLE: What the fuck did you do to him?!

CAMMIE: I don't know, I don't know, I don't know!!!

KYLE: Did he touch you?

CAMMIE: What? Yes. I mean no.

KYLE: Cammie, did he or did he not touch you?

CAMMIE: Yes.

KYLE: He put his fucking hands on you?

CAMMIE: Yes, but it was okay, I swear. It was just a game.

(KYLE *rushes* VICTOR *who has gone into shock on the sofa, a grin on his face.* KYLE *chokes him.* VICTOR *laughs.* KYLE *pulls him off the sofa, continues choking him behind the sofa on the floor.*)

CAMMIE: Kyle! Kyle, stop it! Kyle!!!

(CAMMIE *turns, runs out of the house.* KYLE *continues choking* VICTOR, *then grabs one of the championship belts and starts to beat* VICTOR's *head in.* BOBBY BIBBY *looks on.* VICTOR's *legs stop moving, the belt bloody.* AUNT BOBBIE *appears at the foot of the stairs in her pajamas, turns and sees* KYLE *behind the sofa. They stare at each other as lights fade to black.*)

END OF PLAY

.

www.ingramcontent.com/pod-product-compliance
Lightning Source LLC
Chambersburg PA
CBHW070025110426
42741CB00034B/2568